Ritual of the Daughters of the American Revolution

Ritual

OF THE

Daughters of the American Revolution

PREPARED BY

Mrs. EMMA WAIT AVERY

BELLEVUE CHAPTER, ST. ALBANS, VT.

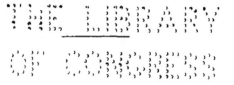
The Fort Hill Press
SAMUEL USHER
176 TO 184 HIGH STREET
BOSTON, MASS.

Copyright secured,
FEBRUARY, 1903.

SUGGESTIONS

———

This Ritual may be easily adapted to the various D. A. R. meetings :

1. Used in its entirety at the regular Chapter, State, National meetings, Washington's Birthday, Flag Day, Fourth of July, or on any public occasion.

2. Shortened by omitting the music, using only the religious, historical, and patriotic responsive readings.

3. Using only the religious part at the beginning and ending of the Ritual.

Chapters having no Chaplain, the Regent can serve in that capacity, or some member can be appointed to act as Chaplain, *pro tem.*

———

Note. — The use of the new national hymn, "Sound Forth again the Nation's Voice," was kindly granted for this Ritual by the authors — the words, Col. Thomas Wentworth Higginson, and the music, Dr. C. Crozat Converse.

D. A. R. RITUAL

REGENT.— Daughters, we meet to honor the memory of our ancestors, to renew our pledge of loyalty to our country and our flag, and to emphasize the privilege and duty of patriotism

CHAPLAIN.— O! Give thanks unto the Lord; call upon His name; make known His deeds among the people.

RESPONSE.—**In Thy name shall they rejoice all the days, and in Thy righteousness shall they be exalted.**

CHAPLAIN.— Seek the Lord and His strength, seek His face evermore.

RESPONSE — **Remember His marvelous works that He hath done.**

CHAPLAIN.— The Heaven, even the Heavens, are the Lord's.

RESPONSE.—**But the earth hath He given to the children of men.**

CHAPLAIN — Praise the Lord, O! Jerusalem; praise the Lord, O! Zion

RESPONSE — **For He hath strengthened the bars of thy gates. He hath blessed thy children within thee.**

CHAPLAIN.— He shall judge among the nations, and shall rebuke many people, and they shall beat their swords into plowshares and their spears into pruning hooks.

RESPONSE.— He maketh wars to cease unto the ends of the earth. He breaketh the bow and cutteth the spear in sunder. Nation shall not lift up sword against nation, neither shall they learn war any more.

CHAPLAIN.— The Lord will give strength unto His people. The Lord will bless His people with peace

RESPONSE.— Whereas thou hast been forsaken and hated, I will make thee an eternal excellency,—a joy of many generations.

Prayer

CHAPLAIN.— Almighty God, Maker of Heaven and earth, we humbly bow before Thee with thanksgiving for the gift of Thy Son, who brought life and immortality to light in the Gospel, and who gave us the principles of freedom, liberty, and righteousness. We give thanks for our country, wherein these principles may be exemplified, and for the valor, devotion, and sacrifice, even unto death, of our ancestors, whose memories we revere.

We thank Thee for Thy sustaining grace and strength during testing times of poverty, sorrow, and affliction. We thank Thee this was not endured in vain, but through them Thou didst preserve our land and endue with the same spirit of fidelity and heroism the successive generations.

We thank Thee for Thy sovereign care, protection, and leadership in the days shadowed with trouble, and that Thou didst give us strength, courage, and guidance, and didst bring in a period of benign peace. We pray Thee to make us steadfast in the cause of human rights and liberty, of law and order, of social justice and national rectitude. And as the spirit of war has been quenched, so that

no longer brother strives against brother, may Thy rich
blessing rest upon us as a nation, and make us Thy people,
tender and patient in charity, resolute and firm for the
right !

Merciful God, our Father, Thou who turnest the hearts of
the children to the Fathers, we thank Thee for the inspira-
tion which called this Patriotic Society into existence, and
we pray Thee to teach us both as a nation, and as an
organization, that fraternity whose love shall abide, that
charity ever fruitful of good works, that loyalty both true
to our country's flag and supremely devoted to the Cross,
the symbol of our faith.

Do Thou so protect our nation that unto the latest genera-
tion its spirit and policy shall be to educate and Christianize
its citizens, to bless all humanity, and to further Thy Holy
Kingdom.

" And finally, when we shall have served Thee in our gen-
eration, may we be gathered unto our Fathers, having the
testimony of a good conscience in favor with Thee, our
God, and in perfect charity with all the world.   All which
we ask through Jesus Christ our Lord."

RESPONSE.— **Amen and Amen.**

SINGING (Page 10). — "**Sound Forth again the Nation's
Voice.**"

REGENT — Our country stands before the world to-day a
    memorial of God-given principles, centuries ago planted in
    the hearts of men across the waters. For the perpetua-
    tion and exercise of these principles, those men, defying
    wind and wave, traversed an unknown sea, and landed upon
    the inhospitable shores of this continent. Then followed,
    at great cost of life, long, wearisome years spent in battling

with an untried climate, subduing forests, wild beasts, and the uncivilized red man. Only God was witness of the toil and hardships, the pain and sorrow endured; but, despite the manifold obstacles, indomitable industry, perseverance, and faith in Almighty God enabled them to achieve mastery; and homes were made, villages, towns, and cities arose.

RESPONSE.— **For the Lord will not cast off His People, neither will He forsake His inheritance.**

REGENT.— And still further must our heroic forefather colonists be tested. Red-handed war must arbitrate relative to national allegiance. Nine long years must dangers be encountered, privations endured, hardships borne, to settle forever the dominance of our land by the Anglo-Saxon.

RESPONSE.— **Blessed is that nation whose God is the Lord, and the people whom He hath chosen for an inheritance.**

REGENT.— Scarce had the demon of war departed and white-winged peace brooded over the colonies, when ominous darkness arose in the horizon. 'T was the Mother Country's hand laid heavily upon the young colonists in unjust demands. The ties of affection were strong, and love and patience had their perfect work, until, finding their remonstrances unheeded, petitions ignored, and prayers unanswered, —

RESPONSE.— **They cry unto the Lord in their trouble, and He bringeth them out of their distresses.**

REGENT.— They arose in the dignity and might of an injured people, a just cause, and an Almighty God, and gave to the world a

DECLARATION OF INDEPENDENCE.

SINGING (Page 14). — **"Hail, Columbia."**

REGENT.— Memory enshrines those brave souls who left happy, prosperous homes, and made their breasts a barricade between our country and its foes, — the long years of poverty, privation, and hardship, the toil of long, weary marches; intense suffering in camp and on bloody field, their fearful sacrifice, not even counting life dear unto themselves, all for God, home, and country.   Such was the price of our liberty.

SINGING (Page 17) — **"Battle Hymn of the Republic."**

REGENT.— Hence, as Daughters of the American Revolution, endeavoring to freshly embalm the memory of this patriotic self-sacrifice, we hope to serve the country for which they fought and died, by encouraging a more zealous and abiding patriotism in the hearts and life of every American citizen.   For we know this example has been perpetuated by the sacrifice of all that men hold dear, both in defense of rights against foreign invaders and when brother rose against brother in fratricidal strife, to uphold the integrity and unity and maintain the power and glory of our American Republic.

RESPONSE.— **Happy is that people whose God is the Lord.**

REGENT.— Realizing that the safety of our country lies in the intelligence, moral character, and patriotism of her citizens, and that the home is where these elements can best be engendered and fostered, as mothers, wives, sisters, our solemn duty is to keep the altar fires of domestic affection and brotherly love blazing on our hearthstones, thus continuing a nation of happy homes, — the highest type of Heaven.

SINGING (Page 22). — **"Home, Sweet Home."**

RESPONSE.— **And for this we give our hands, our heads, our hearts, to our God, our country, and our flag. One God, one country, and one flag. (Salute flag.)**

SINGING (Page 20). — **"The Star-Spangled Banner."**

CHAPLAIN.— Bring ye all the tithes into the storehouse, that there may be meat in mine house, and prove me now herewith, saith the Lord of Hosts, if I will not open you the windows of Heaven and pour you out a blessing that there shall not be room enough to receive it.

RESPONSE.— **And all nations shall call ye blessed, for ye shall be a delightsome land, saith the Lord of Hosts.**

Prayer

CHAPLAIN.— "God of our Fathers, known of old,
Lord of our far-flung battle line,
Beneath whose awful hand we hold
Dominion over palm and pine,
Lord God of Hosts, be with us yet,"

RESPONSE.— **"Lest we forget. Lest we forget."**
Amen and Amen.

SINGING (Page 19) — "America."

SOUND FORTH AGAIN THE NATION'S VOICE.

. (Old Hundred, p. 11.)

THOMAS WENTWORTH HIGGINSON.   C. CROZAT CONVERSE.

ff Choral style and March time.

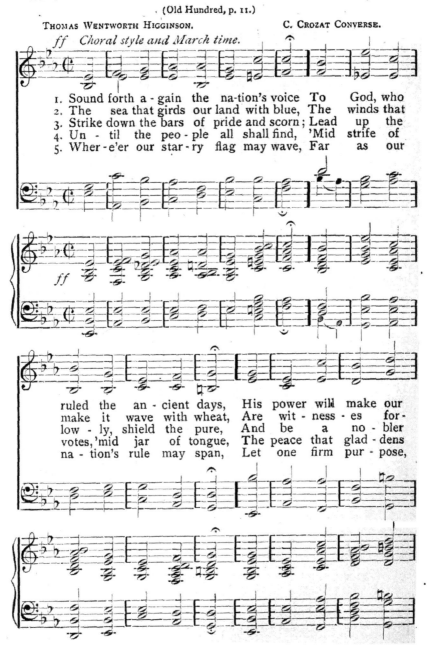

1. Sound forth a - gain the na-tion's voice To God, who
2. The sea that girds our land with blue, The winds that
3. Strike down the bars of pride and scorn; Lead up the
4. Un - til the peo - ple all shall find, 'Mid strife of
5. Wher - e'er our star - ry flag may wave, Far as our

ff

ruled the an - cient days, His power will make our
make it wave with wheat, Are wit - ness - es for-
low - ly, shield the pure, And be a no - bler
votes, 'mid jar of tongue, The peace that glad - dens
na - tion's rule may span, Let one firm pur - pose,

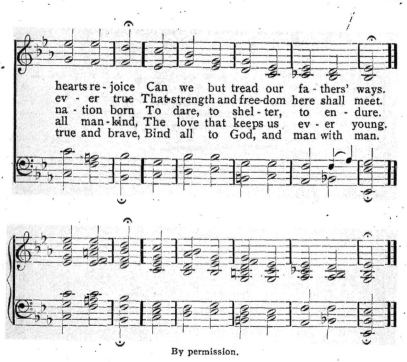

hearts re-joice Can we but tread our fa-thers' ways.
ev - er true That strength and free-dom here shall meet.
na - tion born To dare, to shel-ter, to en - dure.
all man-kind, The love that keeps us ev - er young.
true and brave, Bind all to God, and man with man.

By permission.

OLD HUNDRED.

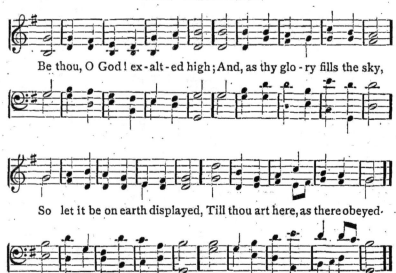

Be thou, O God! ex-alt-ed high; And, as thy glo-ry fills the sky,

So let it be on earth displayed, Till thou art here, as there obeyed.

RED, WHITE, AND BLUE.

Written and composed by DAVID T. SHAW.

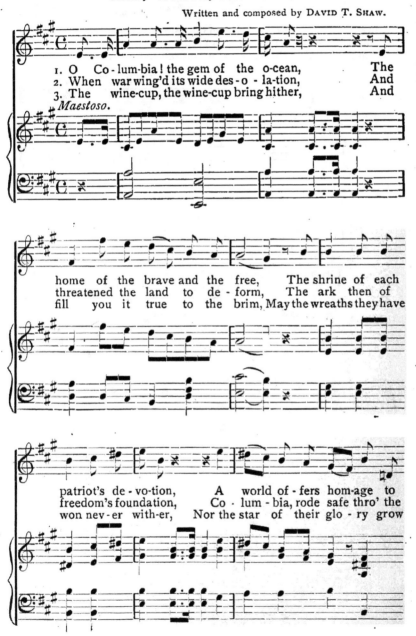

1. O Co-lum-bia! the gem of the o-cean,   The
2. When war wing'd its wide des-o-la-tion,   And
3. The wine-cup, the wine-cup bring hither,   And

Maestoso.

home of the brave and the free,   The shrine of each
threatened the land to de-form,   The ark then of
fill you it true to the brim, May the wreaths they have

patriot's de-vo-tion,   A world of-fers hom-age to
freedom's foundation,   Co-lum-bia, rode safe thro' the
won nev-er with-er,   Nor the star of their glo-ry grow

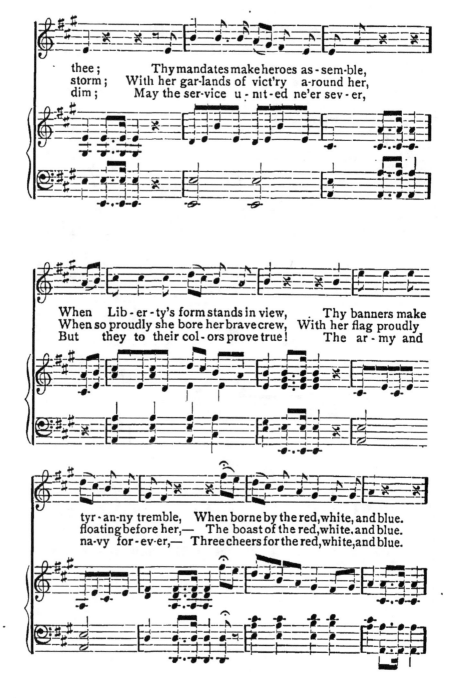

thee ; Thy mandates make heroes as-sem-ble,
storm ; With her gar-lands of vict'ry a-round her,
dim ; May the ser-vice u-nit-ed ne'er sev-er,

When Lib-er-ty's form stands in view, Thy banners make
When so proudly she bore her brave crew, With her flag proudly
But they to their col-ors prove true! The ar-my and

tyr-an-ny tremble, When borne by the red, white, and blue.
floating before her,— The boast of the red, white, and blue.
na-vy for-ev-er,— Three cheers for the red, white, and blue.

CHORUS.

When borne by the red, white, and blue, When borne by the red, white, and blue,
The boast of the red, white, and blue, The boast of the red, white, and blue,
Three cheers for the red, white, and blue, Three cheers for the red, white, and blue,

Thy banners make tyranny tremble, When borne by the red, white, and blue.
Her flag floating proudly before her, The boast of the red, white, and blue.
The army and navy forever, Three cheers for the red, white, and blue.

HAIL, COLUMBIA.

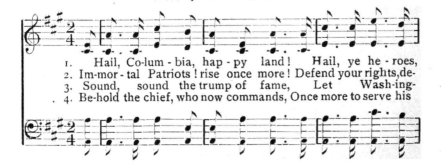

1. Hail, Co-lum-bia, hap-py land! Hail, ye he-roes,
2. Im-mor-tal Patriots! rise once more! Defend your rights, de-
3. Sound, sound the trump of fame, Let Wash-ing-
4. Be-hold the chief, who now commands, Once more to serve his

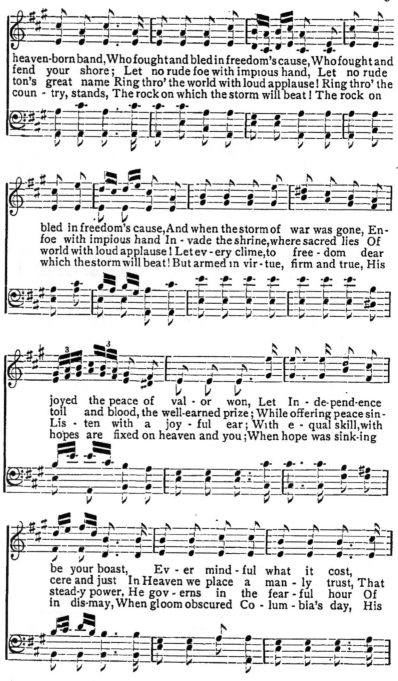

heaven-born band, Who fought and bled in freedom's cause, Who fought and
fend your shore; Let no rude foe with impious hand, Let no rude
ton's great name Ring thro' the world with loud applause! Ring thro' the
coun - try, stands, The rock on which the storm will beat! The rock on

bled in freedom's cause, And when the storm of war was gone, En-
foe with impious hand In - vade the shrine, where sacred lies Of
world with loud applause! Let ev - ery clime, to free - dom dear
which the storm will beat! But armed in vir - tue, firm and true, His

joyed the peace of val - or won, Let In - de-pend-ence
toil and blood, the well-earned prize; While offering peace sin-
Lis - ten with a joy - ful ear; With e - qual skill, with
hopes are fixed on heaven and you; When hope was sink-ing

be your boast, Ev - er mind - ful what it cost,
cere and just In Heaven we place a man - ly trust, That
stead-y power, He gov - erns in the fear - ful hour Of
in dis-may, When gloom obscured Co - lum - bia's day, His

Ev - er grate - ful for the prize,   Let its al - tar
truth and jus - tice may pre-vail,   And ev - ery scheme of
hor - rid war, or guides with ease,   The hap - pier time of
stead - y mind, from changes free,   Resolved on death or

reach the skies   Firm u - ni - ted let us be,
bon - dage fail.   Firm u - ni - ted let us be,
hon - est peace.   Firm u - ni - ted let us be,
Lib - er - ty.   Firm u - ni - ted let us be,

Rally - ing round our lib - er - ty! As a band of

broth - ers join'd, Peace and safe - ty we shall find.

BATTLE HYMN OF THE REPUBLIC.

Words by JULIA WARD HOWE.

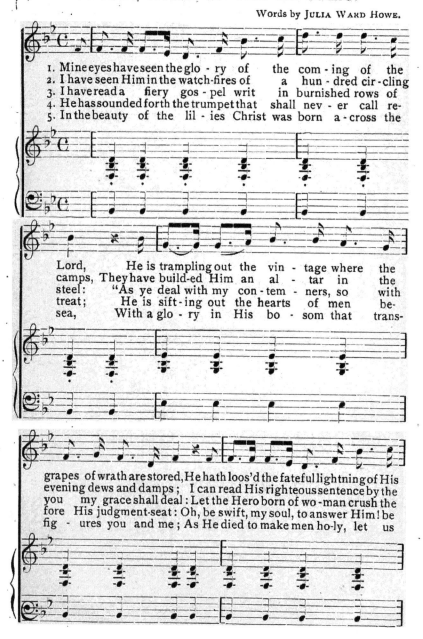

1. Mine eyes have seen the glo - ry of the com - ing of the
2. I have seen Him in the watch-fires of a hun - dred cir - cling
3. I have read a fiery gos - pel writ in burnished rows of
4. He has sounded forth the trumpet that shall nev - er call re-
5. In the beauty of the lil - ies Christ was born a - cross the

Lord, He is trampling out the vin - tage where the
camps, They have build-ed Him an al - tar in the
steel: "As ye deal with my con - tem - ners, so with
treat; He is sift - ing out the hearts of men be-
sea, With a glo - ry in His bo - som that trans-

grapes of wrath are stored, He hath loos'd the fateful lightning of His
evening dews and damps; I can read His righteous sentence by the
you my grace shall deal: Let the Hero born of wo - man crush the
fore His judgment-seat: Oh, be swift, my soul, to answer Him! be
fig - ures you and me; As He died to make men ho-ly, let us

ter-ri-ble swift sword : His truth is marching on.
dim and flaring lamps : His day is marching on.
ser-pent with his heel, Since God is marching on.
ju - bi-lant, my feet ! Our God is marching on.
die to make men free, While God is marching on.

f CHORUS.

Glory ! Glory ! Hal-le-lu-jah !   Glory ! Glory ! Glory ! Hal-le-lu-jah !

Glory ! Glory ! Hal-le-lu - jah !   His truth is marching   on.
Glory ! Glory ! Hal-le-lu - jah !   His day is marching   on.
Glory ! Glory ! Hal-le-lu - jah ! Since God is marching   on.
Glory ! Glory ! Hal-le-lu - jah !   Our God is marching   on.
Glory ! Glory ! Hal-le-lu - jah ! While God is marching   on.

AMERICA.

S. F. SMITH.

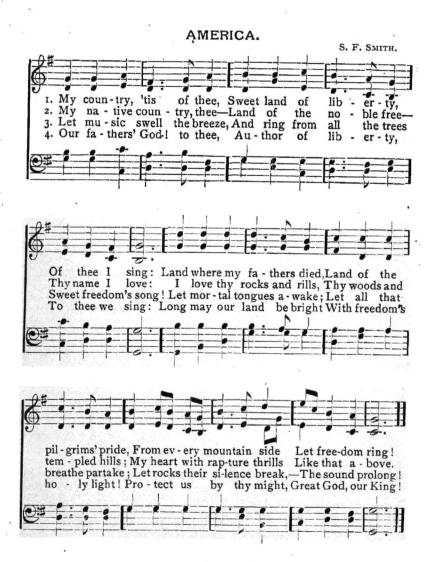

1. My coun-try, 'tis of thee, Sweet land of lib - er - ty,
2. My na - tive coun - try, thee—Land of the no - ble free—
3. Let mu - sic swell the breeze, And ring from all the trees
4. Our fa - thers' God! to thee, Au - thor of lib - er - ty,

Of thee I sing: Land where my fa - thers died, Land of the
Thy name I love: I love thy rocks and rills, Thy woods and
Sweet freedom's song! Let mor - tal tongues a - wake; Let all that
To thee we sing: Long may our land be bright With freedom's

pil - grims' pride, From ev - ery mountain side Let free-dom ring!
tem - pled hills; My heart with rap-ture thrills Like that a - bove.
breathe partake; Let rocks their si-lence break,—The sound prolong!
ho - ly light! Pro - tect us by thy might, Great God, our King!

THE STAR-SPANGLED BANNER.

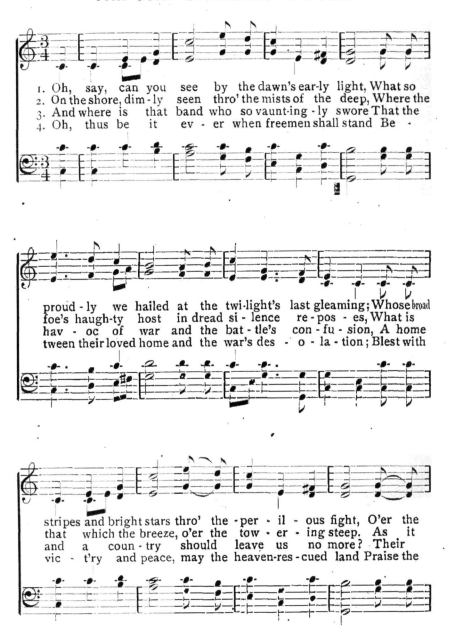

1. Oh, say, can you see by the dawn's ear-ly light, What so
2. On the shore, dim-ly seen thro' the mists of the deep, Where the
3. And where is that band who so vaunt-ing-ly swore That the
4. Oh, thus be it ev - er when freemen shall stand Be -

proud - ly we hailed at the twi-light's last gleaming; Whose broad
foe's haugh-ty host in dread si - lence re - pos - es, What is
hav - oc of war and the bat - tle's con - fu - sion, A home
tween their loved home and the war's des - o - la - tion; Blest with

stripes and bright stars thro' the -per - il - ous fight, O'er the
that which the breeze, o'er the tow - er - ing steep, As it
and a coun - try should leave us no more? Their
vic - t'ry and peace, may the heaven-res - cued land Praise the

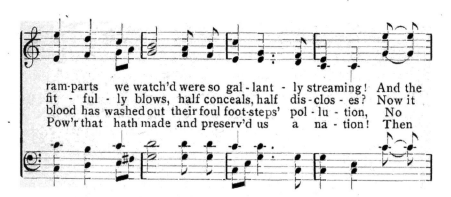

ram-parts   we watch'd were so gal-lant - ly streaming! And the
fit - ful - ly blows, half conceals, half dis-clos - es? Now it
blood has washed out their foul foot-steps' pol - lu - tion, No
Pow'r that hath made and preserv'd us   a   na - tion! Then

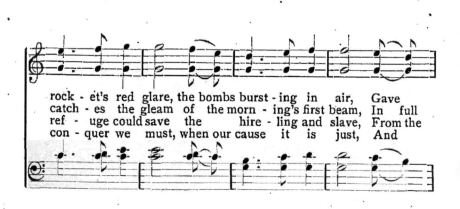

rock - et's red glare, the bombs burst-ing in   air,   Gave
catch - es the gleam of the morn - ing's first beam, In   full
ref - uge could save the   hire - ling and slave, From the
con - quer we must, when our cause it is   just, And

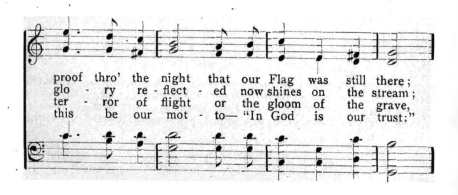

proof thro' the night that our Flag was still there;
glo - ry   re - flect - ed now shines on   the stream;
ter - ror of flight or the gloom of the grave,
this   be our mot - to— "In God is our trust;"

Oh! say, does that Star-Span-gled Ban - ner yet wave,
'Tis the Star-Span - gled Ban - ner—Oh, long may it wave,
And the Star-Span - gled Ban - ner in tri - umph doth wave,
And the Star-Span - gled Ban - ner in tri - umph doth wave,

O'er the land of the free and the home of the brave?
O'er the land of the free and the home of the brave!
O'er the land of the free and the home of the brave.
While the land of the free is the home of the brave!

HOME, SWEET HOME.

Andante.

1. 'Mid. pleas-ures and pal - a - ces, though we may roam,
2. An ex - ile from home, splendor daz - zles in vain,
3. How sweet 'tis to sit 'neath a fond fath - er's smile,
4. To thee I'll re - turn, o - ver-bur-den'd with care,

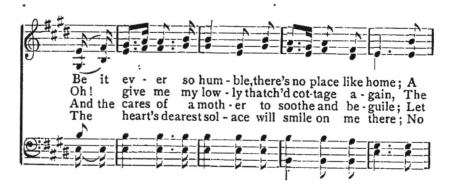

Be it ev - er so hum - ble, there's no place like home; A
Oh! give me my low - ly thatch'd cot-tage a - gain, The
And the cares of a moth - er to soothe and be - guile; Let
The heart's dearest sol - ace will smile on me there; No

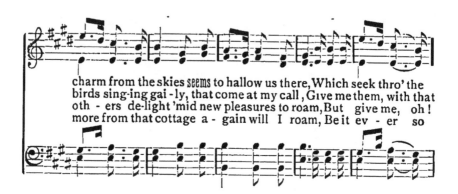

charm from the skies seems to hallow us there, Which seek thro' the
birds sing-ing gai - ly, that come at my call, Give me them, with that
oth - ers de-light 'mid new pleasures to roam, But give me, oh!
more from that cottage a - gain will I roam, Be it ev - er so

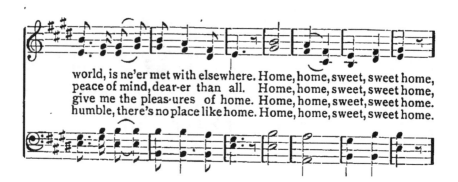

world, is ne'er met with elsewhere. Home, home, sweet, sweet home,
peace of mind, dear-er than all. Home, home, sweet, sweet home,
give me the pleas-ures of home. Home, home, sweet, sweet home.
humble, there's no place like home. Home, home, sweet, sweet home.

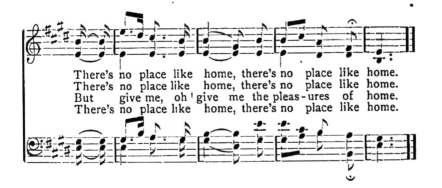

There's no place like home, there's no place like home.
There's no place like home, there's no place like home.
But give me, oh give me the pleas-ures of home.
There's no place like home, there's no place like home.